This little book is dedica
weapon of choice to protect it.

Alien Birthday Cake

Poor Little Thing

Seeing Double Trouble

Crawling With Rats

Target Practice

Do Not Open

Blood And Guts

There's Something In Your Hair

Possessed Kitchen Utensil

Nightmare In The Water

Frozen Body Parts

Witch's Brew

Zombie Frogs

I Lost A Nail

Doorway To Hell

Pirate's Curse

What's That Noise

Leaking Package

Playful Piranha

Voodoo Doll

Hungry For Love

Web Of Bones

The Doctor Is In

Rotting Teeth

Prehistoric Menace

Creepy Footprints

Vampire Heart

Machete At Work

Bloody Rags

Rabid Turtle

Madness Within

Path To The Portal

Library Of Souls

Alien Terrarium

Chained Melody

Shark Food

Kill It With Fire

You In 75 Years

Devil's Toy Box

Worst Deadly Sin

Shattered Glass

When Food Fights Back

Bulbous Globs

Padded Cell

Snakes On A Brain

Stab In The Dark

Slimy Fingers

Worms Crawling Out

Foaming At The Mouth

All Stitched Up

Poe Would Be Proud

Trapped In Limbo

Not Entirely Human

Let's Play A Game

Foul Breath

Borderline Psycho

Blinded By Fright

Made The Cut

Shadow Monster

One Doesn't Belong

Cave Dweller

Battle Scars

Hypodermic Poison

Holy Water Cure

Mirrors Reflecting Evil

Mummy Can Dance

Charred Remains

Demon Bride

Grinning Skull

Spinal Tap

It's Behind You

Busting Out

Creature Of Habit

Puddles Of Goo

That Which Is Hidden

Cemetery Visitor

Dungeon Floor

How Everything Ends

Made in United States
Orlando, FL
13 December 2021